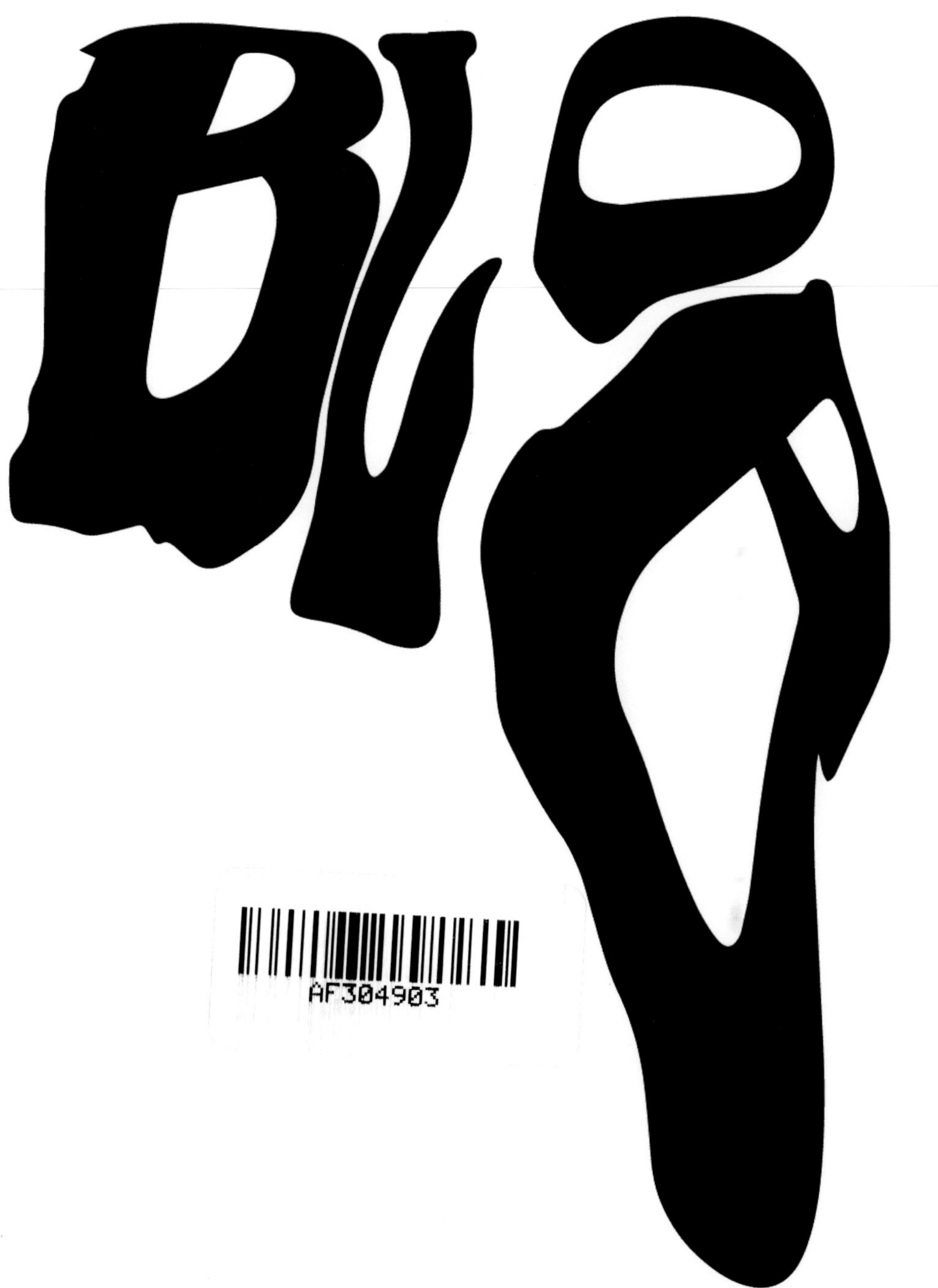

BLO

Eddy Frankel

TROLLEY

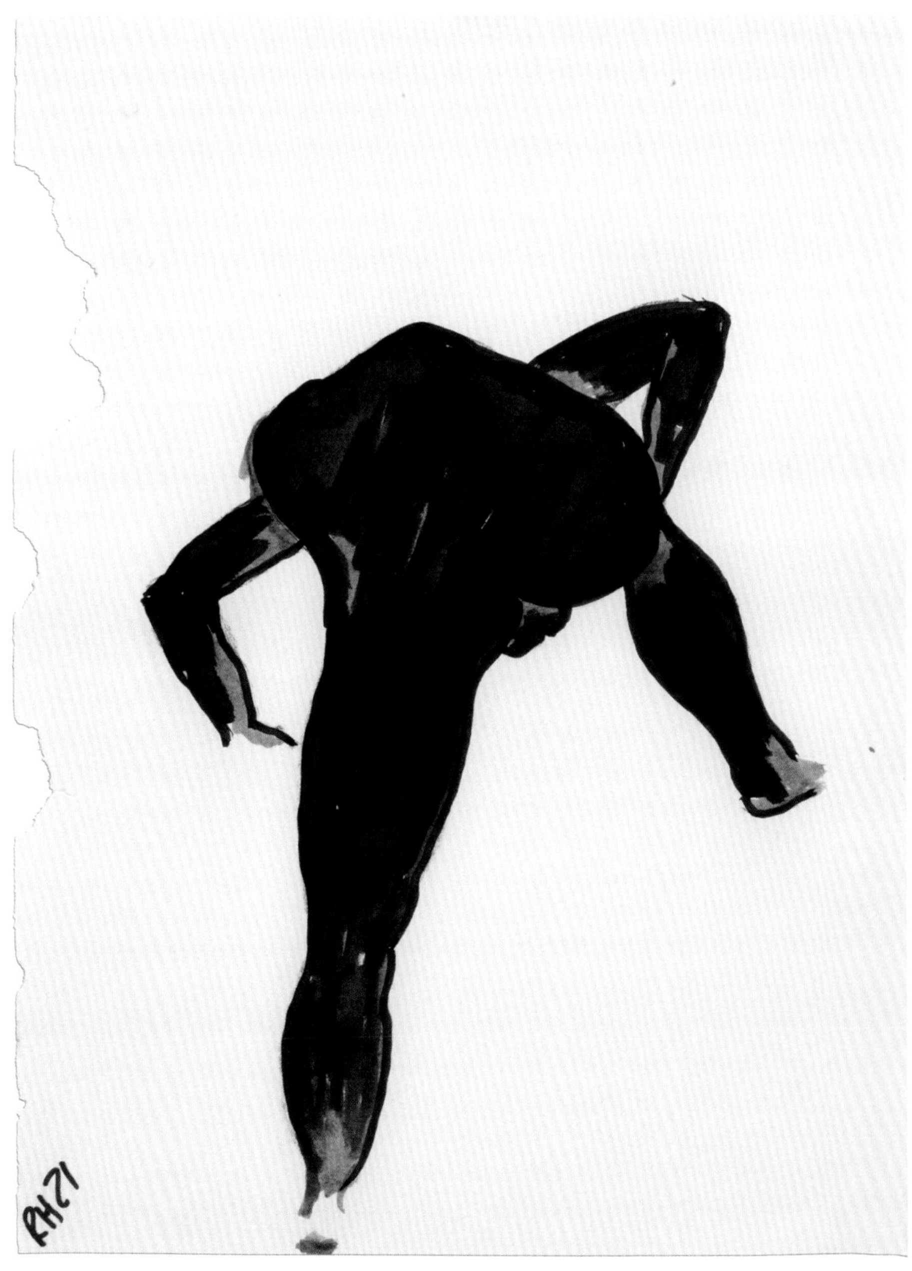

I became a blob slowly. The transformation from functional adult man to oozing, boneless, gelatinous mass didn't happen overnight, but over the course of months and years. So slowly you could barely tell it was happening. You don't notice changes when you live with them day to day. It's only with big slippages of time that things become horrifyingly, grossly, formlessly apparent. You stumble across an old driving licence or a photo from some teenage party and, fucking hell, you had a jawline, piercing eyes and waves of hair; you remember you had vitality, passion and erections – oh god, erections that would never end.

That disconnect between the pristine past and the cracked present has the same shock as watching a bowl of fruit left to rot in time lapse or images of deforestation in the Amazon. Look at what we have lost, look at what we have become. Feel shame.

I live that life in extremis. My changes were slow, almost imperceptible, like something geological, the melting of a glacier.

It started like any unctuous slide into your 30s. The gentle, autumnal, creeping follicular nudity of hair loss, the gathering of weight around the belly like space junk coagulating in orbit around a dying planet. Some men age, most decompose. Clooney, better looking at 50 than 20. The rest of us? We just flub and flab and melt and moult until we look like haunted versions of our younger selves. Real-life portraits of Dorian Gray that have leeched off the canvas to invade your towns and cities.

But it wasn't just age with me. It was misery. You can read people's joy in their bodies. Happy people look happy: unfurrowed, glowing, like sunshine leaks out of every orifice. Fucking unbearable. Misery does the opposite.

Stress and anxiety and depression and sadness erode your features. Worry lines around the mouth, creases across the brow, the sag of sullen cheeks. Chewed, stubby nails; sunken, tired, grey eyes. You're shaped physically by your mental state. That's why I'm a blob.

Oh god, I wish it was just age. I wish it was just male pattern baldness and a gentle paunch, bones getting creakier, organs turning to mush. But I'm the physical result of countless mental neuroses, of social anxiety, of depression, of guilt, of years and years of accumulated shame. You eat garbage, it clogs your arteries. You think garbage, it clogs your brain, and then – it turns out – your body. Hate yourself enough

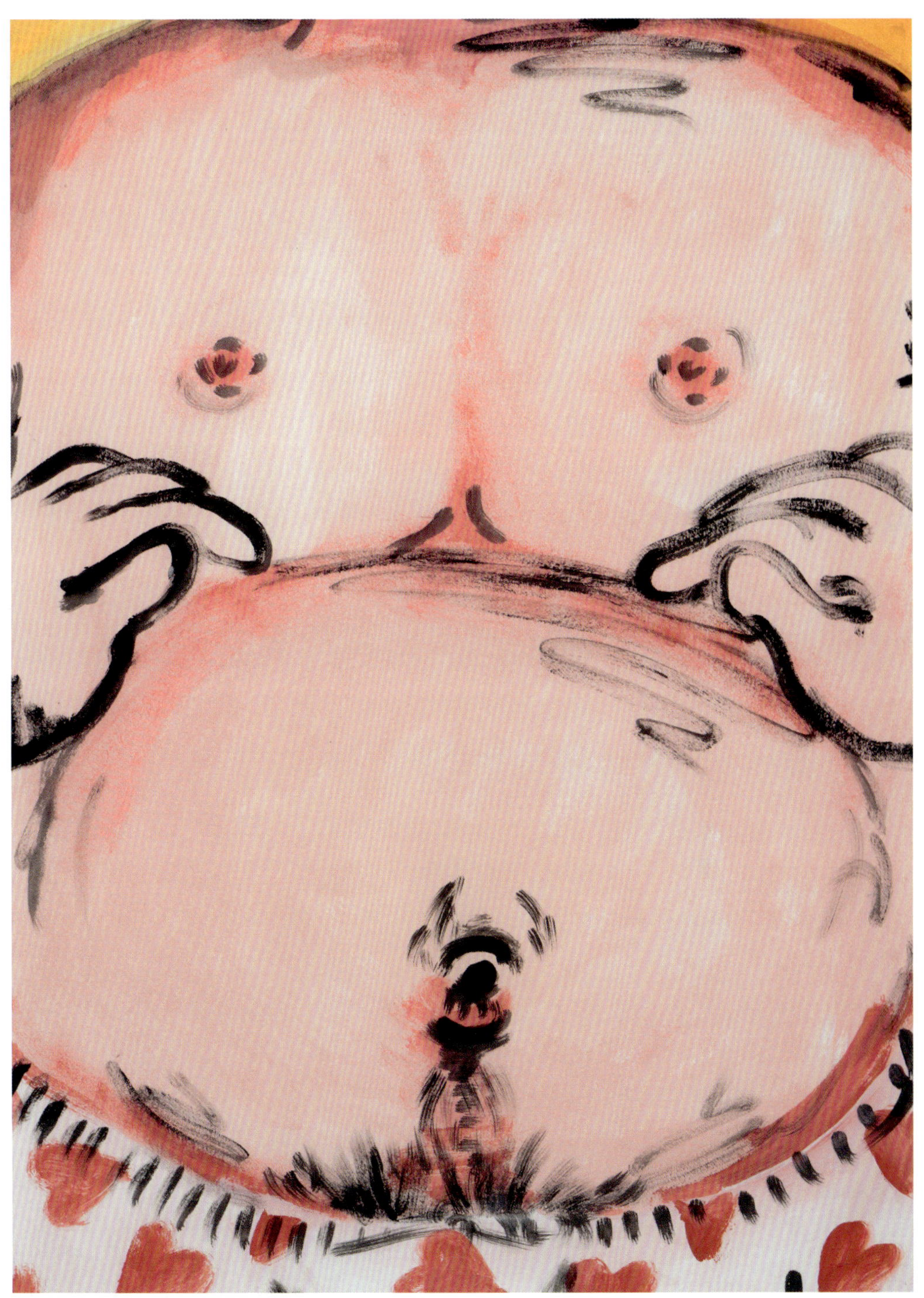

and you can destroy yourself. It's not a hugely useful superpower, but it's better than nothing, I guess.

I still have limbs, a torso, a face, all the usual bits of a human body, but my bones have long since dissipated, just crumbled and melted away, leaving only musculature and fibre and cartilage and fat and orifices. I slip and slide, I expand to fill any space, part-man, part-liquid. I decalcified, they tell me. My bones turned to jelly, then to dust. It was painless. For months my piss was milky as the material of my frame expunged itself from my body. My semen became thick and gloopy, like lumpy custard.

It comes from everywhere, the misery. I used to stare at myself shirtless in the bathroom mirror, hands cupped around my little proto-paunch. Squeeze and twist down

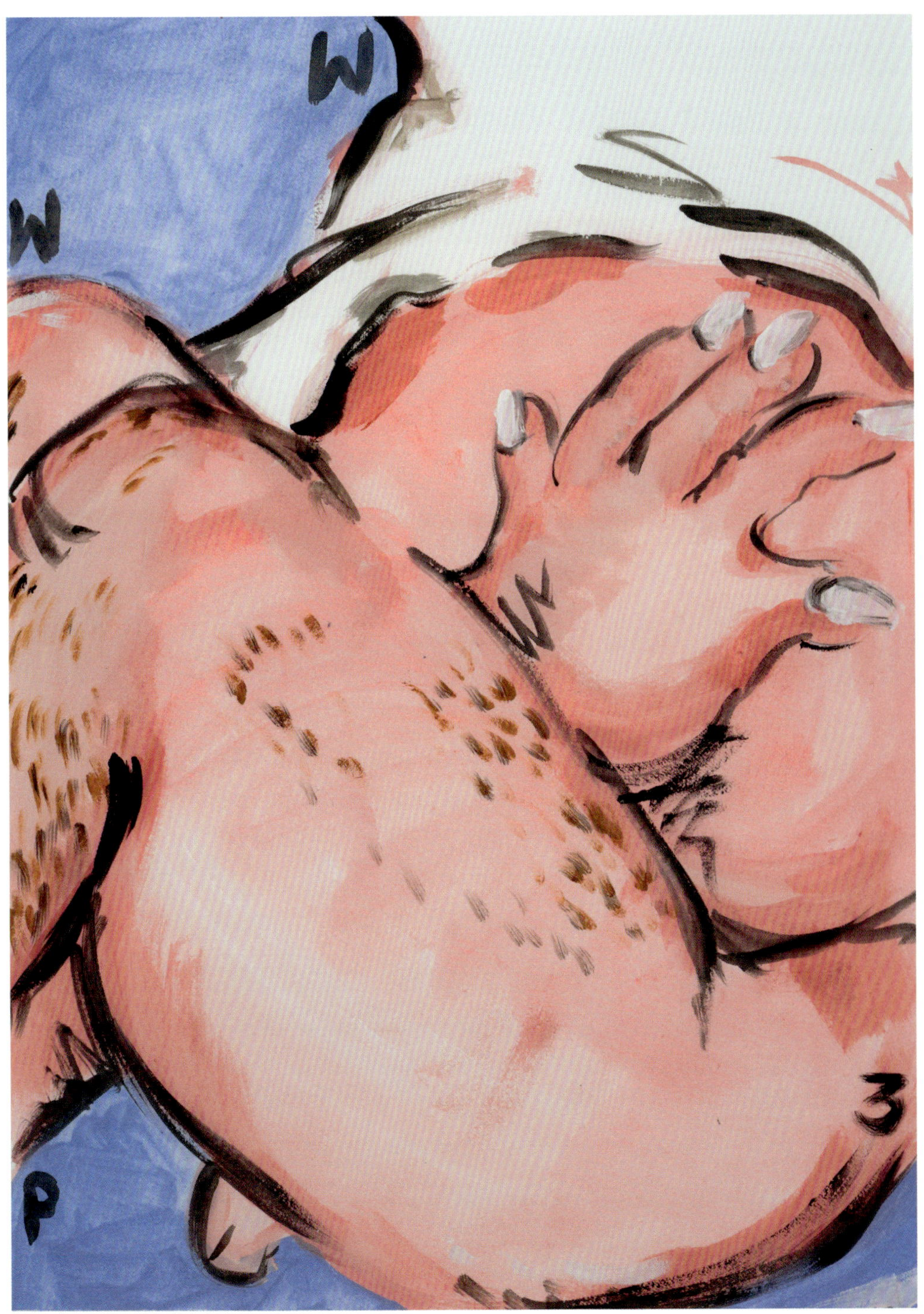

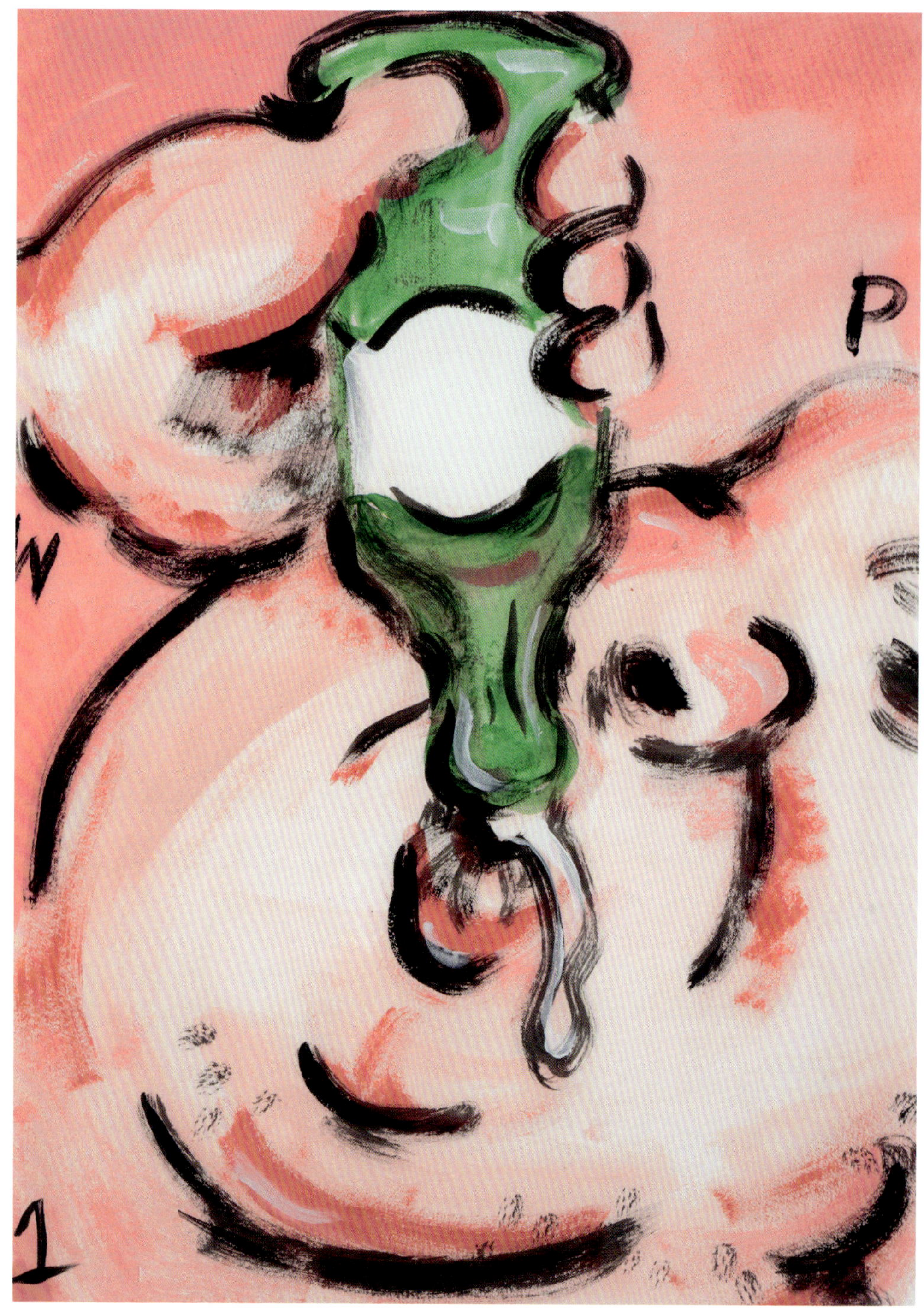

P
W
1

Olivia Sterling

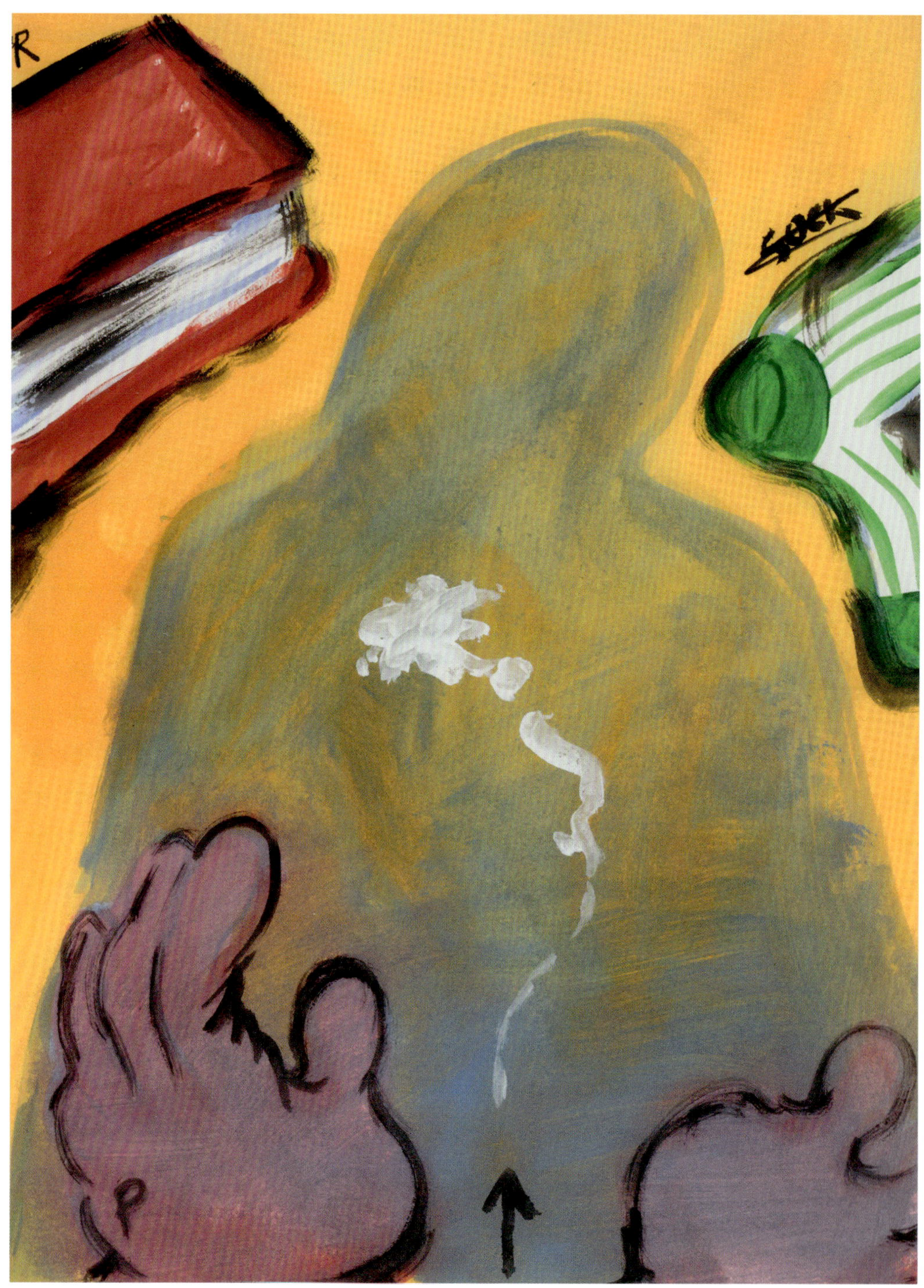

and your belly button creases into a cartoon frown, your nipples like forlorn, bloodshot eyes. Squeeze and twist up and it becomes a grimacing grin. Tragedy and comedy, all the hahas and boohoos of life playing themselves out across your torso, a work of Shakespearean brilliance for an audience of one, with the cold tiles of an overlit bathroom as your grand stage.

The misery is like a toupee I've glued on to my head, obvious for everyone to see but too much of a safety blanket for me to dare venture out without. It was a gift, really, from my parents. 'We don't care what you do in life, Frank, as long as you're happy,' they'd say. As long as I'm happy?! There is no greater curse than the love of your parents, than two people telling you that all you have to aim for is happiness, and in doing so ensuring you would always, always miss. I could've been a drug dealing neo-Nazi and these people would've said 'as long as you're happy!' Wishing for someone's happiness, you might as well wish them into an early grave.

Before becoming a blob, I was another mid-30s man with pointless ambitions, witty friends, a drinking habit and a pretty girlfriend. Every night Christine used to slide up against me in bed, embracing me with her whole body, pulling herself close to me. Then a hand would reach over – like the big spoon had grown limbs – and cup my stomach. 'Stop,' I'd say, pulling her hand up to my chest.

'Don't be like that,' she'd reply. 'I love your little belly, it's cute.'

I'd clench my jaw so tightly you could feel the tension throbbing into the pillow. I didn't want to be cute. I wanted to be virile, powerful, confident, attractive, a rock-hard being of muscle and erections and pungent, intoxicating sexuality. 'It's *sexy*,' she'd say, the lie leaking out of *her* like excreta bubbling uncontrollably into a colostomy bag.

Every night the same battle, her invading little hands trying to infiltrate the staunch defence of my arm clenched tight against my body, worming its way towards the site of the beginnings of my own slow deflation.

The belly cupping was an accidental process of emasculation, a subconscious quest to demean and belittle me into a compliant, wet, fetid old man. It's not sexy to fall apart, it's not sexy to age and crumble and wither. But it *is cute*. It is unthreatening. It is the *sign of*

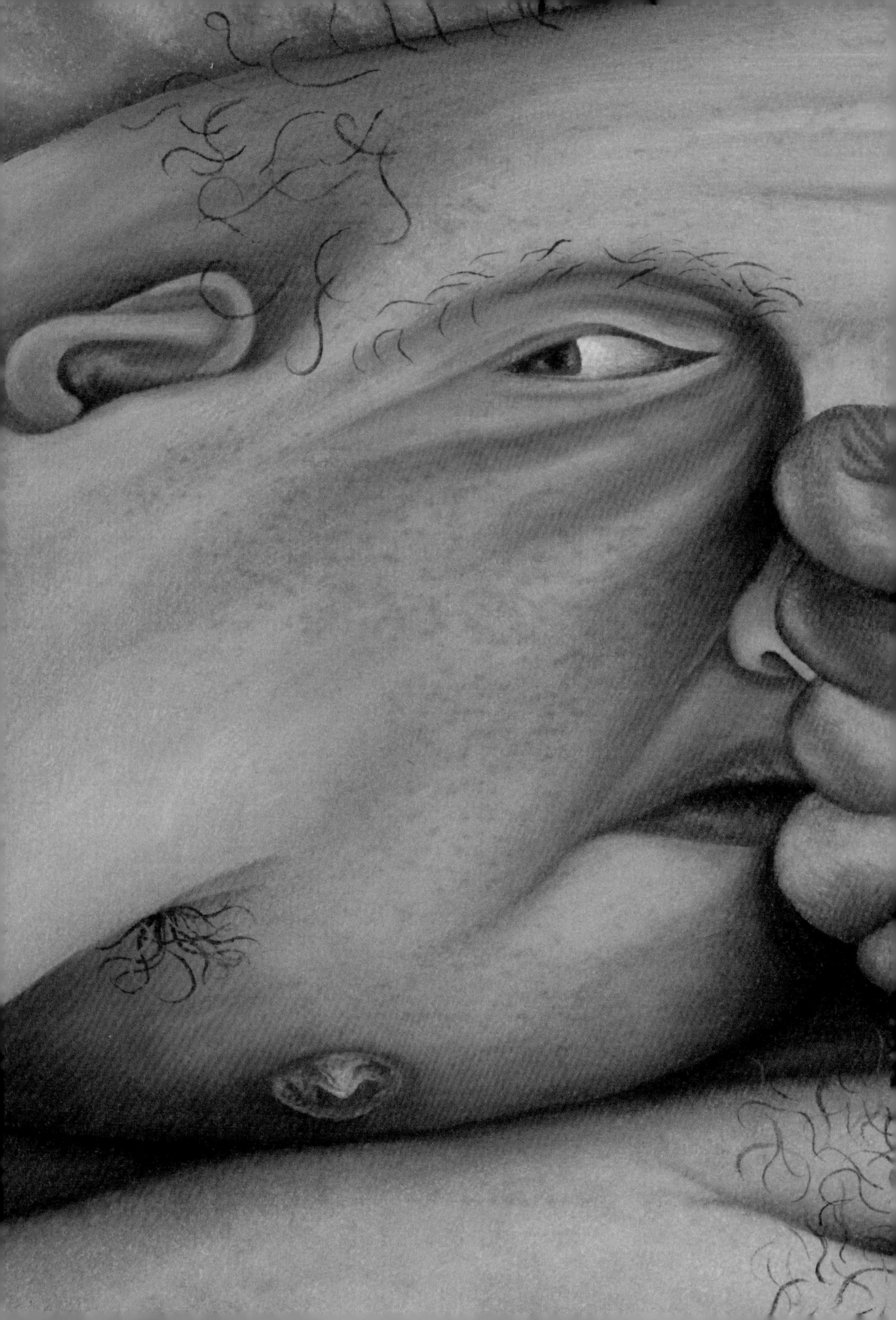

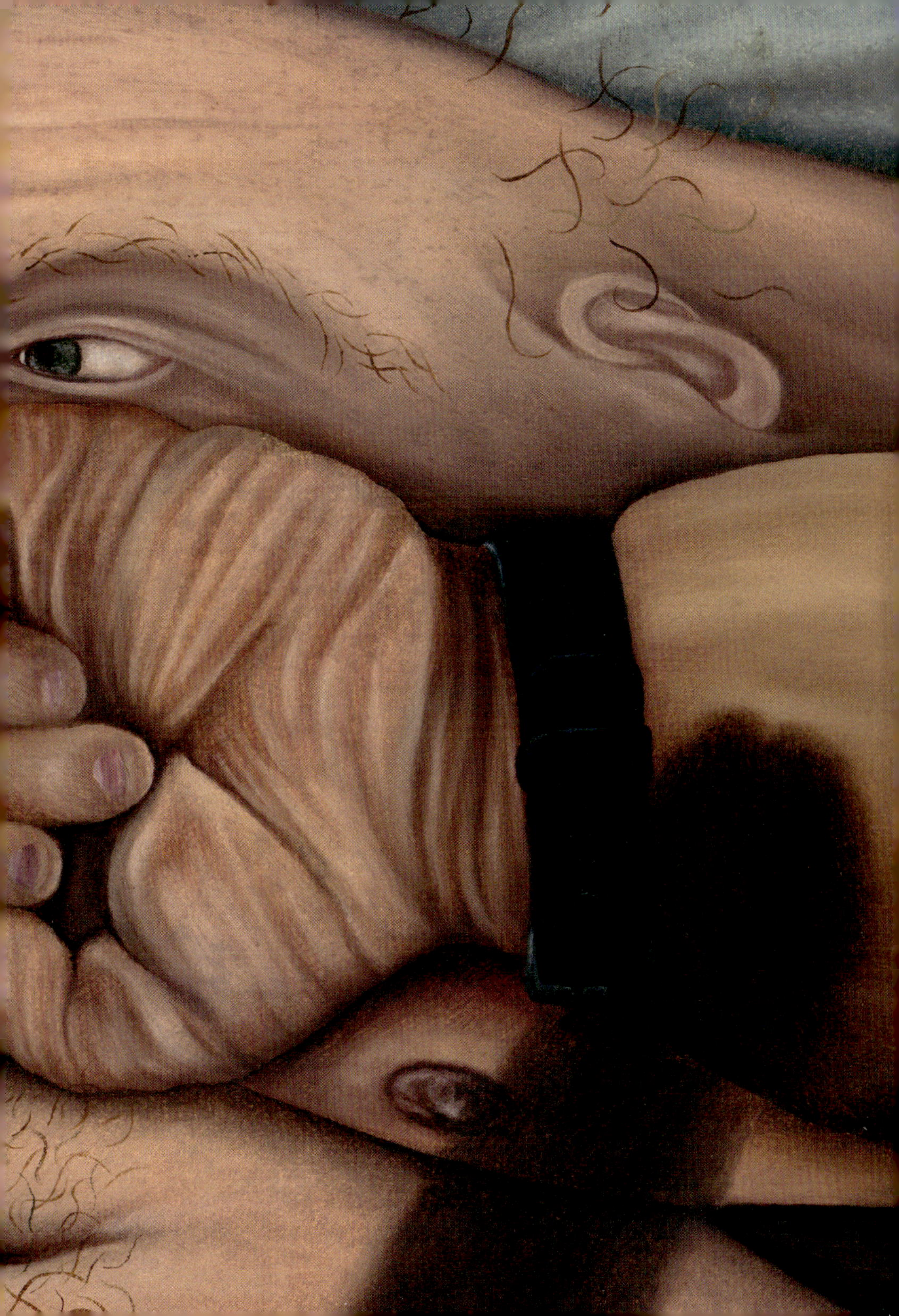

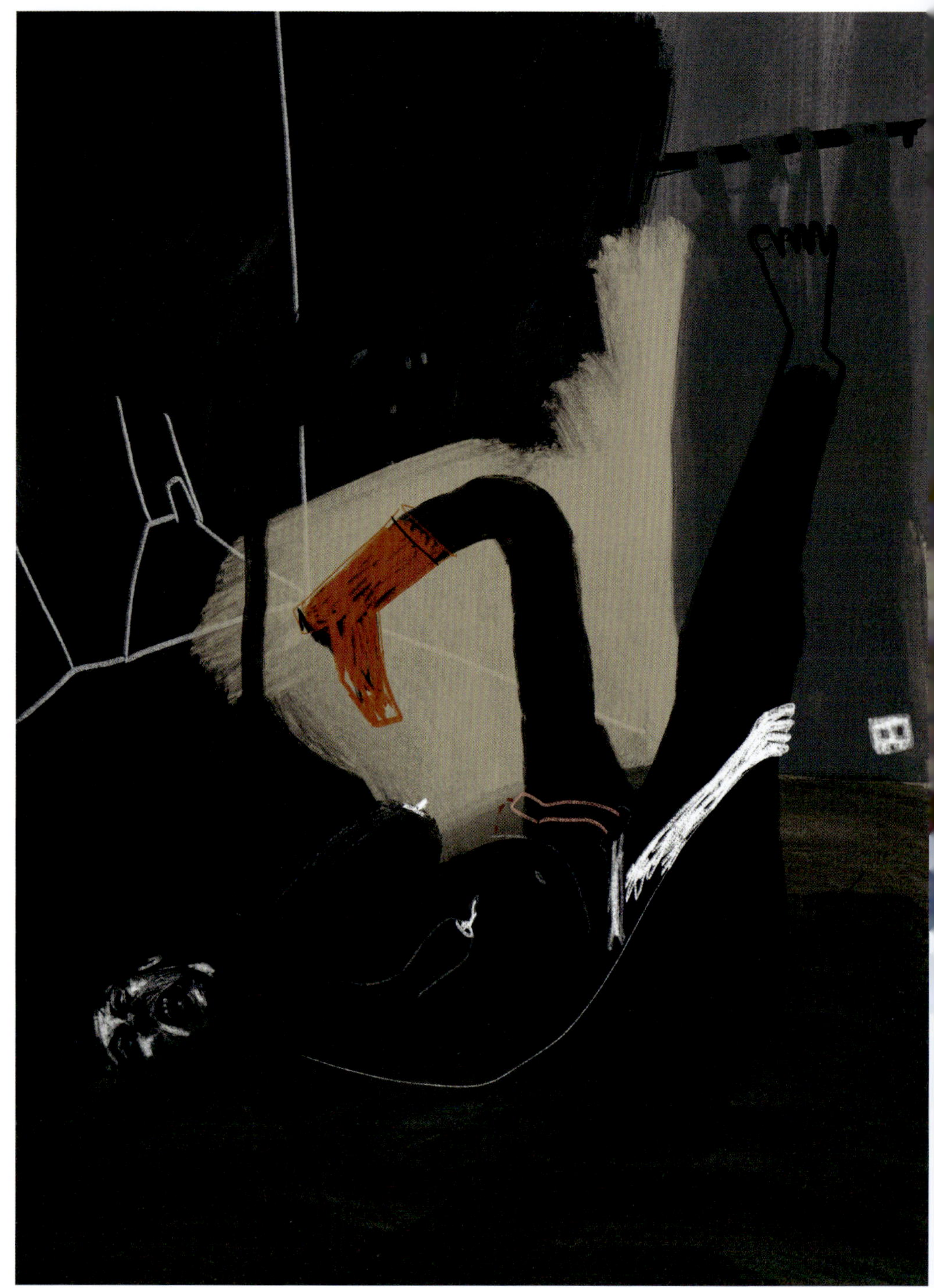

a man beginning to find comfort in life and accepting the onrush of years. Or that's what it should look like. But I can't age gracefully, I can't sink into the slippers of mediocrity with *alacrity* and *charm* and just smirk *my way* kindly through life. And *the worst* thing is I don't even have *the balls* to age disgracefully, with *booze and drugs* and anger and righteousness and rebellion. There's no flight or fright, I'm frozen in the middle, panicking *about my* body while numbing the panic *with booze* and food while panicking *about the* booze and food while *panicking* about the panic itself, *etc etc etc* ad infinitum, ad vomitum, *ad defectum,* etc etc etc.

It's not her fault. She's still perfect, all these years later, Christine. Caring, compassionate, comfortable in her skin. *All* that beautiful, luscious, cascading *blonde* hair that *would* clump in huge knots in the *shower's* plughole, but somehow *never* leave a bald patch on her head. *I resented her* follicular prowess as I balded, *hated how she'd* leave me these sodden, *twisted* creatures in the shower, *taunting* and mocking me with gruesome, *ratty* voodoo dolls aimed at my *own* particular impotence.

She visits me *now,* bringing *little gifts* and kisses *on* the soft, bare patch of skin that *was* once my forehead. She doesn't *call* me cute anymore. I am grotesque, and *she's* too *smart to lie.* We watch Saturday cooking *shows,* or talk about the Tories. *She tells* me about her new lawyer *boyfriend,* their flat in North West London, Kensal somewhere or Willesden something. A *damp* and quiet place to plant their *odious* middle-class roots, for their *blonde,*

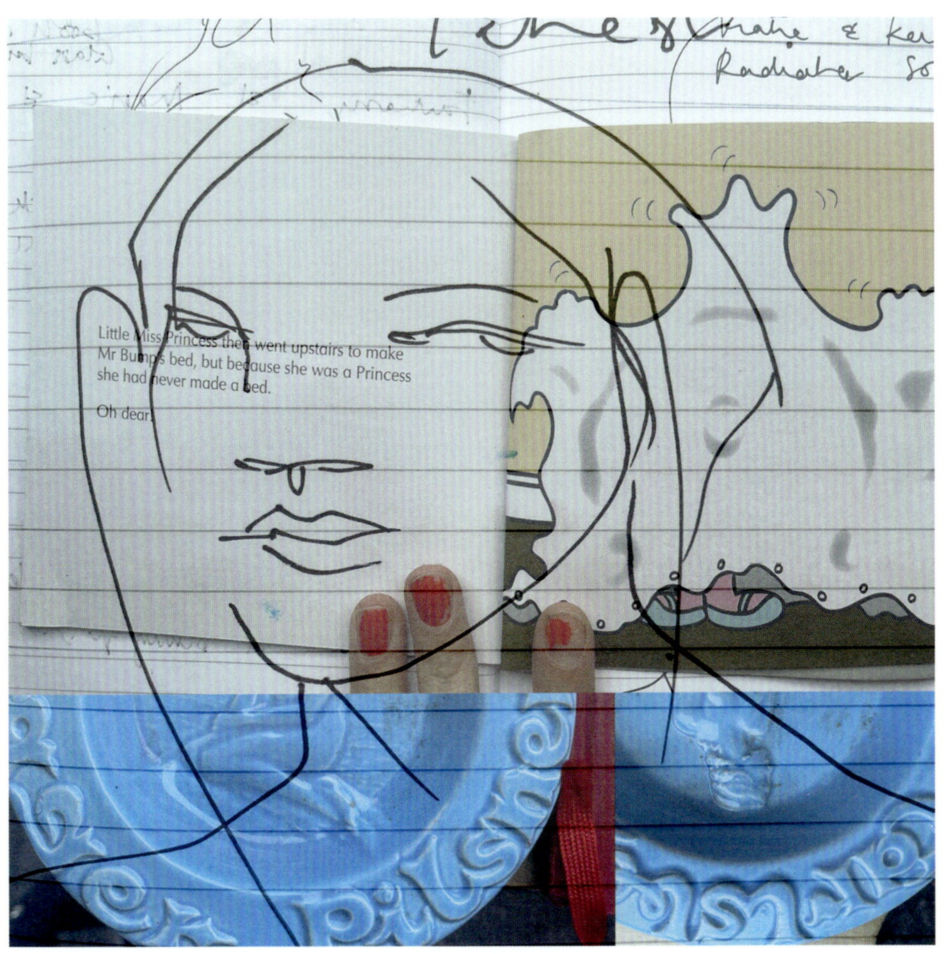
Little Miss Princess then went upstairs to make
Mr Bumps bed, but because she was a Princess
she had never made a bed.

Oh dear!

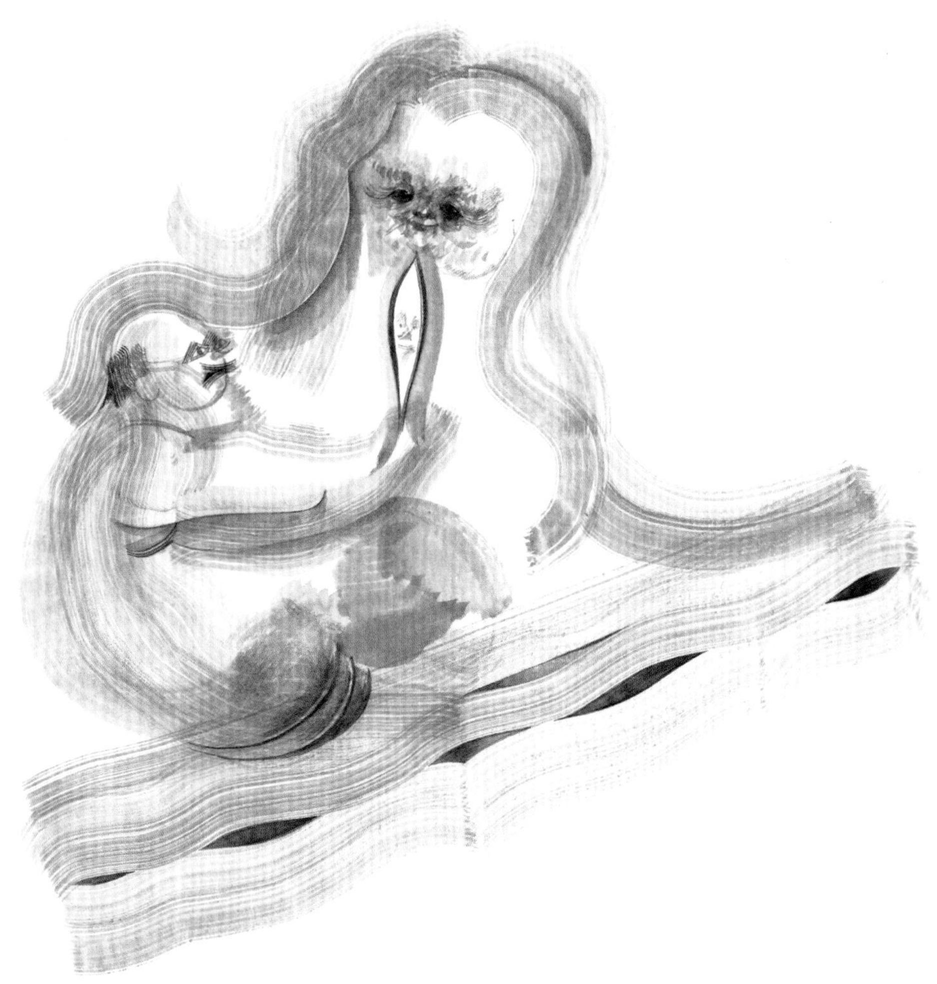

gentile children with vomit-inducing names to commute to their private schools from and blossom into unbearably confident happy adults. You know exactly what Christine will become, how her children will grow and make her proud, how none of them will de-ossify and melt into a blob of grim misery.

She always knows when to leave: just as the smell of my arousal begins to waft up from my scent glands. She can't bear to witness it. Who can blame her.

I mean, I can still get erections. There's no bone in a boner, just throbbing, pulsating blood and musculature. I look like a one-eared space hopper. Tug it enough and the rest of me jiggles, like stirring jelly with a paddle. As the nurses wash me, the arousal floods through my veins, pumping desire across my whole being. As soon as the wet sponge in the gloved hand hits my limpid skin, I become unavoidably engorged. They studiously ignore my member, carefully washing around it like a toxic flagpole they must avoid.

Christine pays for a monthly 'service' for me, a woman or man who specialises in helping the unhelpable, to come take care of my basest needs. They come first thing in the morning for their dirty task, sometimes the same faces, sometimes naïfs, encountering a blob for the first time. 'Where do I start?' they ask the nurses with panic in their voices, fear flickering staccato in their eyes. But before an answer is uttered, the stiffness appears in my world of flaccidity, a slow-saluting sea captain on a sinking ship, and they know. They help, these poor manipulators of flesh. Physically, at

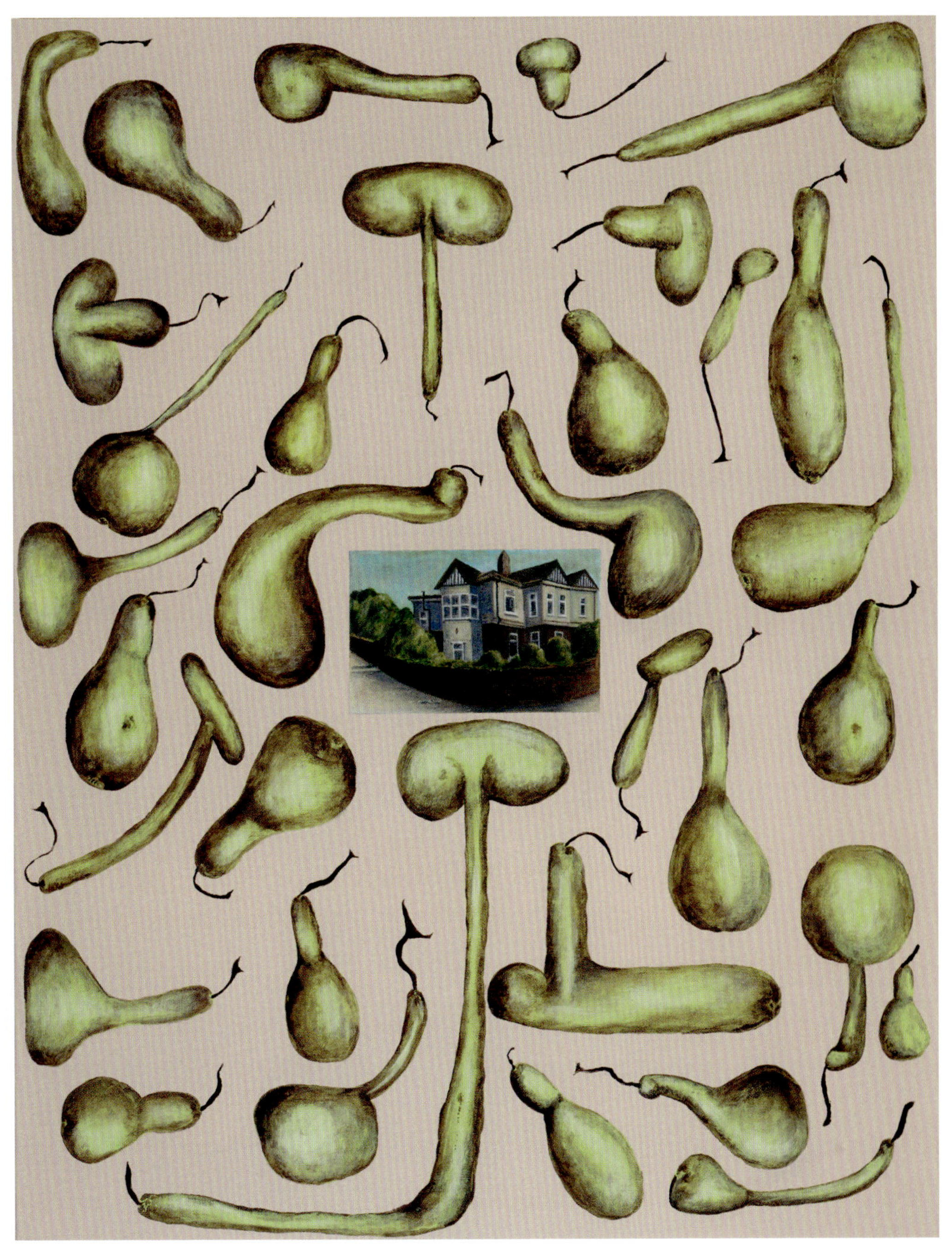

least. They drain the muck from the pipes of my body with their hands or obscene, vibrating, prosthetic vaginas. But they can't drain away the shame of arousal. I mean, arousal is always shameful. Erections are meant to be tucked under your belt; desire is for things you can't have. Imagine arousal when it manifests as a singular solid mass on an otherwise near-liquid body. A mast on a deflated lilo. A rigid reminder of past solidity. Arousal is a hateful, blushing shame at the best of times, but it's much worse as a blob, totally lacking dignity, without even recourse to hiding my throbbing physicality.

The doctors say I'm a miracle. After months of tests and MRIs they remain shruggingly clueless, but ego-strokingly impressed. Your heart shouldn't have the strength to force your blood through a boneless

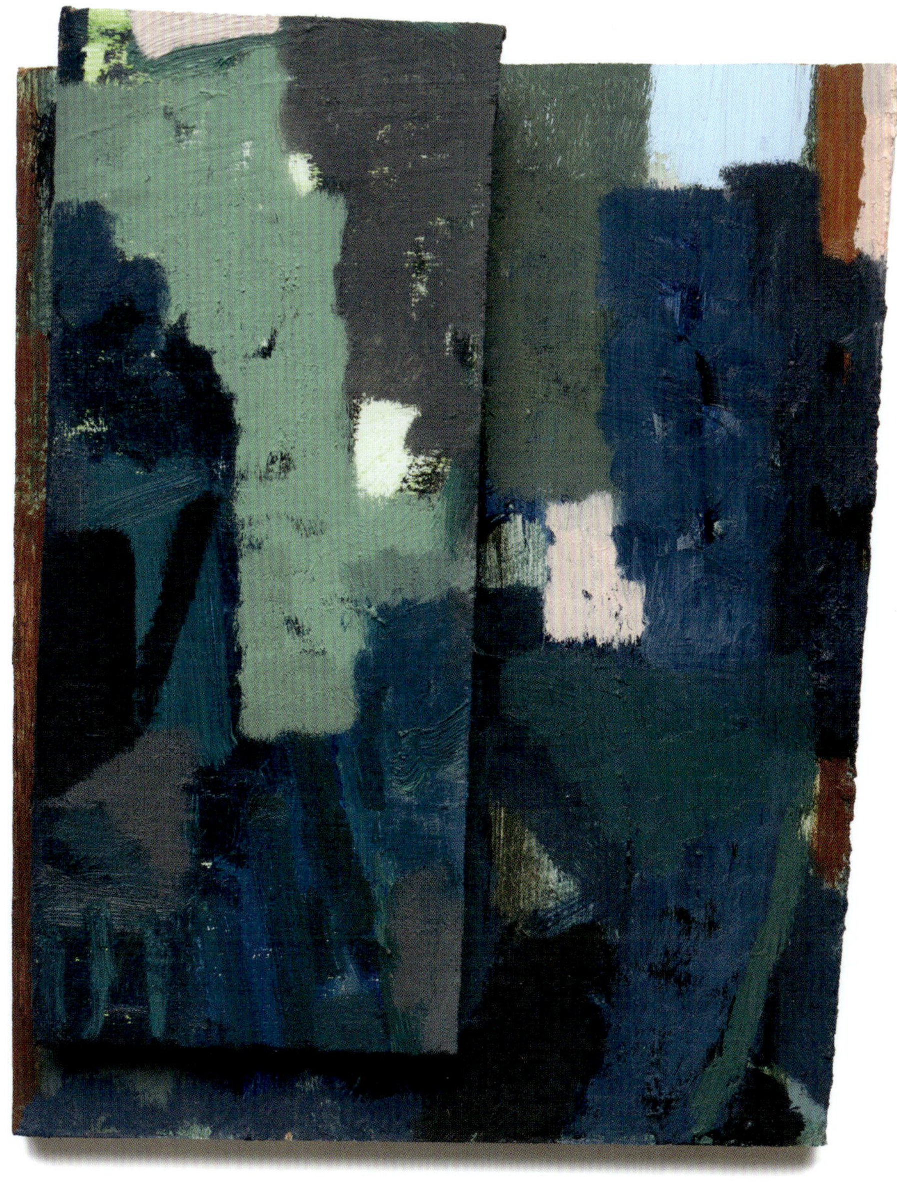

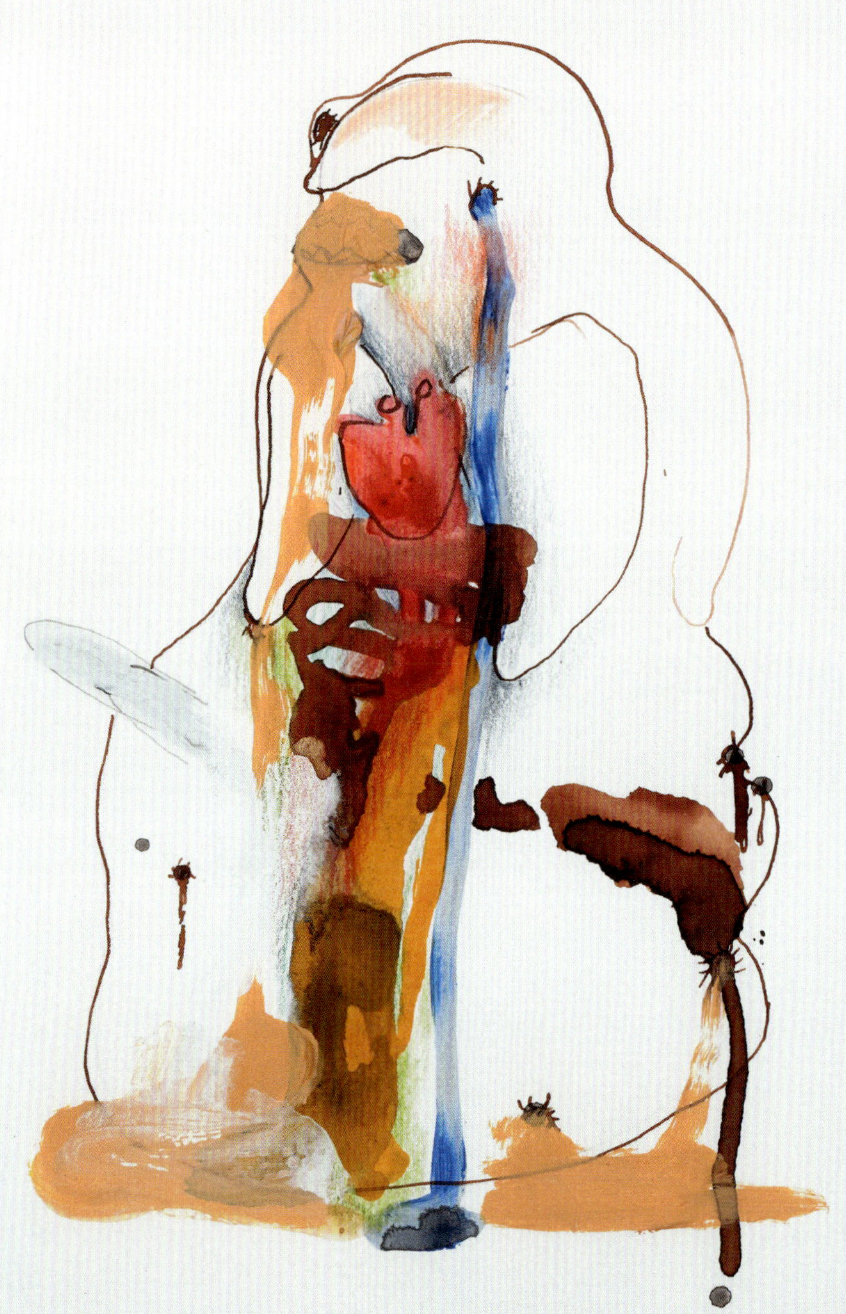

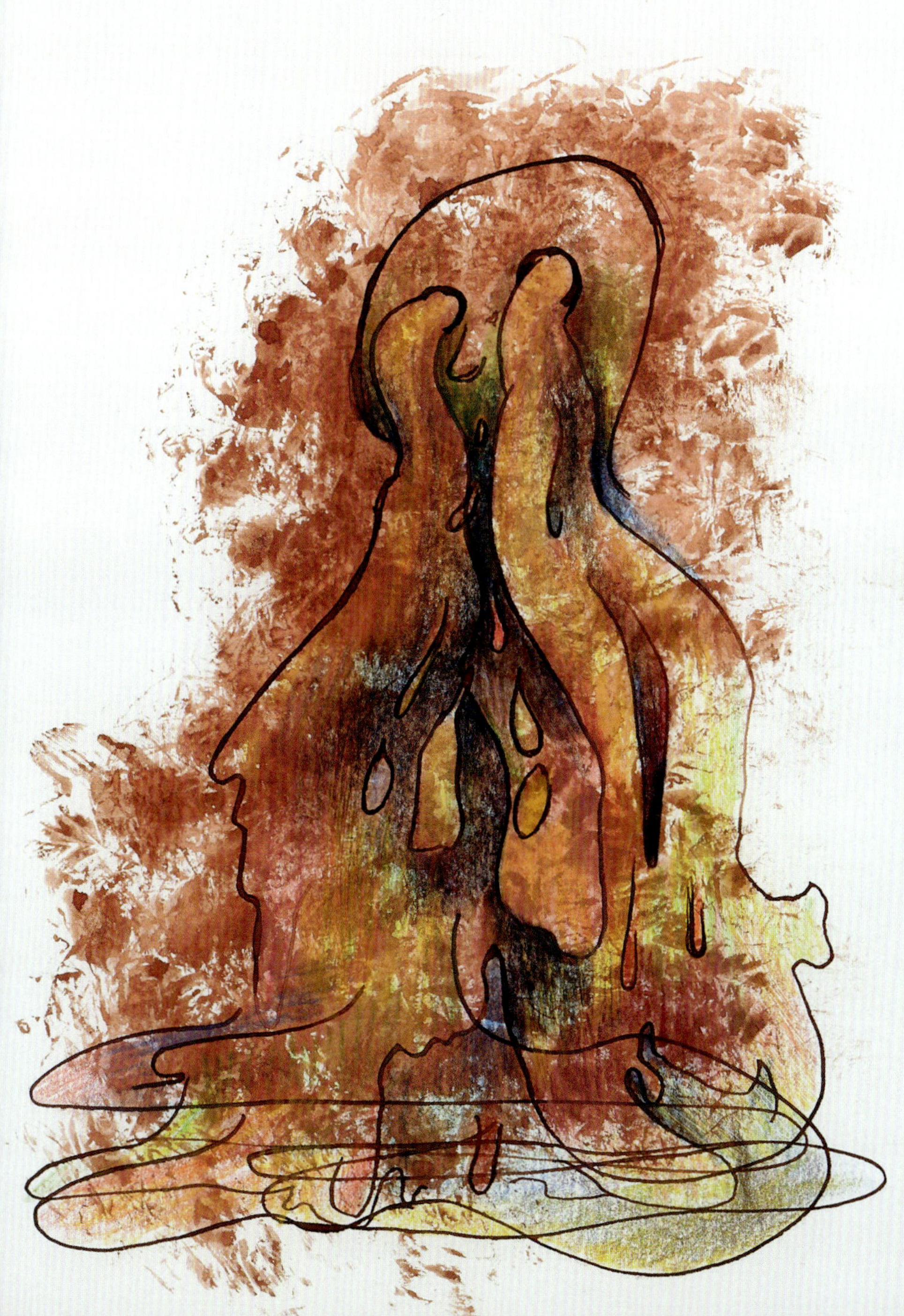

body.' Boneless, like I'm a KFC meal deal.

Frank, it's amazing. Somehow, as you've lost bone density, the rest of your body seems to have taken up the slack. Your heart's enormous, your lungs are powerful and fibrous, your organs are covered in new, tense muscles, you shouldn't be alive, but here you are!'

Here I am. Slinking slowly along the hospital floor, accumulating debris and dust and dirt on my skin like the world's most depressing Roomba.

I undulate off my bed and down the corridors, a gelatinous apparition haunting the doctors and nurses and other patients, sneaking past their doors, rolling through their conversations, making the words catch in their throats as they try to keep their stomachs from turning mid-anecdote. Don't mind me, just a living metaphor for regret, coming through, beep beep.

The nurses find me eventually, haul me onto a trolley and lever me back into bed, reconnecting all the tubes. They leave me to the quiet of an empty room: and in almost every way, it's okay. Life is okay, I mean. There are no goals or aims or next steps or hopes or ambitions, there is only me and the wavy ebbing of existence. And I think, sometimes, that maybe I'm happy.

Then yesterday, I felt a small piece of something solid somewhere along the base of where my spine had once been. In all of my softness, here – somehow – was this speck of solidity. I felt my skin tingle, the goosebumps prickle along my body like countless microscopic erections. It felt like bone. It felt like my bone, *like* my bones were growing back, *like* I was returning to my normal, human state, like I was becoming myself again.

The *tears* started to stream down my face as I realised that the pain and torment of the last few years, the de-ossification of my body, the blobbifying of Frank, was a *lesson*, a ridiculous, overwrought morality play! It was nature's way of making me come to terms with the idea that constantly striving for happiness, always looking to achieve and grow and succeed, was the exact thing stopping me from being happy. That if I just slowed down, maybe, and took life as it came, I would finally find joy! I could be out in weeks, or maybe months, whatever the doctors say. I can wait, a year, two, it doesn't matter. I'll be out! I could walk to Christine's flat in Kensal something

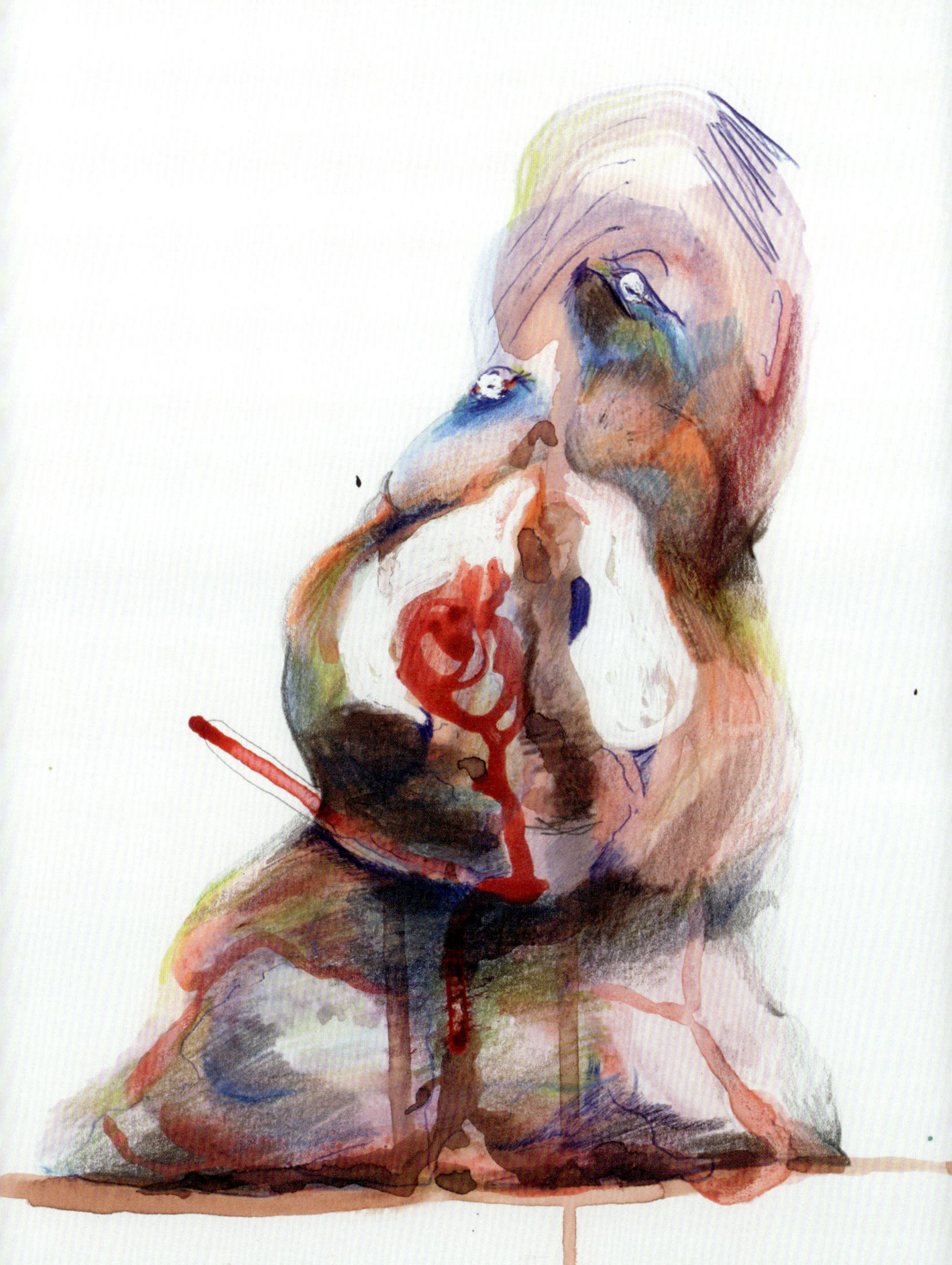

and she'd take me back, it would be our tedious children we'd send off to some unaffordable school every day, it would be our terraced house in some faceless bit of a too-big city, our endlessly repetitive date nights and tasteless dinners, and it would be perfect! It would be happiness! I would be content with it, I wouldn't be unsatisfied or long for new thrills anymore! The tears, you wouldn't believe the tears. I was sodden. 'Nurse', I screamed. 'Nurse! I'm healing, my bones are growing back!' She came running in and I told her breathlessly about the spine that I knew, for certain, was re-growing in my back. She rolled me over gently, more gently than ever before, and placed a latex gloved hand against my back, feeling for the growth. Silence. She rolled me back and lifted her hand, showing me a single AAA battery that had tumbled out of one of my own vibrating pleasure devices, knocked to the floor earlier that day as I glooped out of bed on my way into the ward after a visit from one of Christine's helpers. 'Something you picked up on your travels,' the nurse said, her voice soft and gentle, before leaving me with a smile and a kind wink.

The tears stopped. In an instant, all of my hope and happiness was replaced with pulsing waves of my oldest friend shame. Shame, and abject fear that the nurse didn't put the battery back where it should be, and tomorrow would be utter, and total, misery.

INDEX

BLOB
Eddy Frankel

Images ©
Shadi Al-Atallah
Luke Burton
Gareth Cadwallader
Emma Cousin
Rachel Howard
France-Lise McGurn
Glen Pudvine
Mary Ramsden
Olivia Sterling

Text © Eddy Frankel

Design DR.ME

ISBN 978-1-907112-64-5
Printed in Wales by Gomer Press 2022
Published in Great Britain in 2022 by Trolley Ltd

www.trolleybooks.com